Regina Dahl

Love Is Not Selfish

WestBow Press books may be ordered through booksellers or by contacting:

WestBow Press
A Division of Thomas Nelson & Zondervan
1663 Liberty Drive
Bloomington, IN 47403
www.westbowpress.com
844-714-3454

ISBN: 978-1-4497-9289-3 (sc)
ISBN: 978-1-4497-9290-9 (e)

Library of Congress Control Number: 2013907495

Print information available on the last page.

WestBow Press rev. date: 08/31/2022

Scripture references from: 1 Corinthians 13:4-7 (NLT), 1 John 4:8 (NLT), and Ephesians 5:1&2 (NIV).

WESTBOW
PRESS®
A DIVISION OF THOMAS NELSON
& ZONDERVAN

To the Author of Love; the Lover of my soul —

With special thanks to all who have demonstrated true Love.

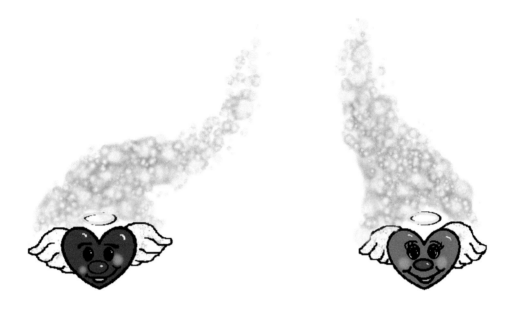

"Hi! Our names are Caleb and Gracie, and we are here to help as you read through this book about love. We will also be back at the end of this book with a special message just for you!"

"Love is patient and kind. Love is not jealous or boastful or proud or rude. It does not demand its own way. It is not irritable, and it keeps no record of being wronged. It does not rejoice about injustice but rejoices whenever the truth wins out. Love never gives up, never loses faith, is always hopeful, and endures through every circumstance."

1 Corinthians 13: 4-7 (NLT).

Love is patient. Love does not rush or force anyone to do anything. Love waits for others and makes time to bless others, because…

…Love is not selfish.

Love is kind. Love does not do mean things to hurt others. Love sees others and cares about them in everything it says and does, because…

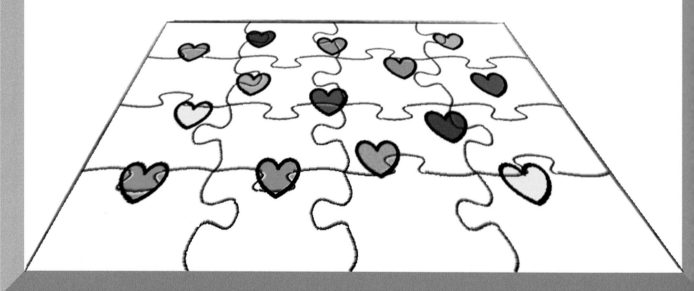

…Love is not selfish.

…Love is not selfish.

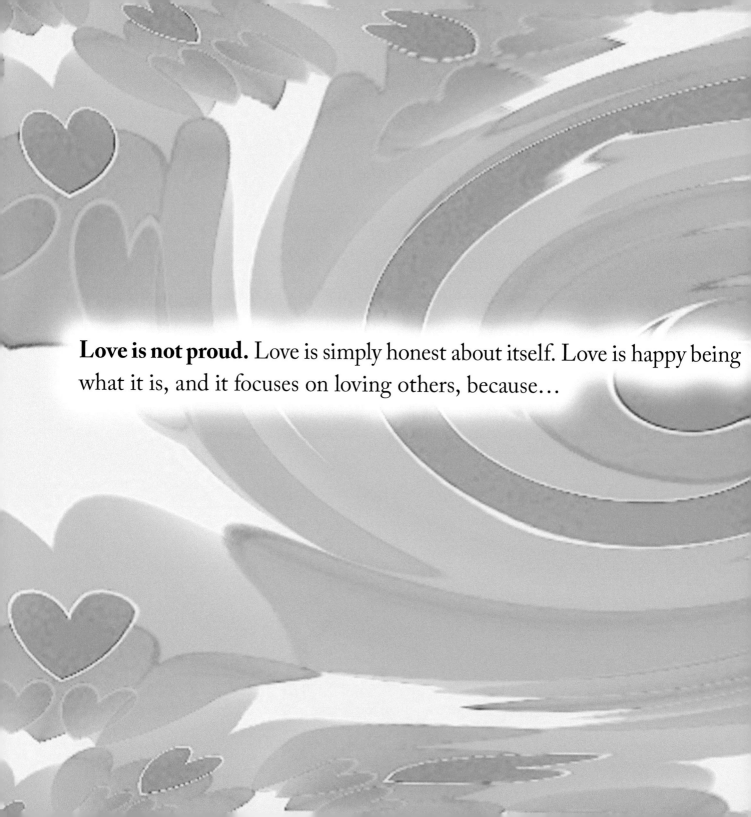

Love is not proud. Love is simply honest about itself. Love is happy being what it is, and it focuses on loving others, because…

...Love is not selfish.

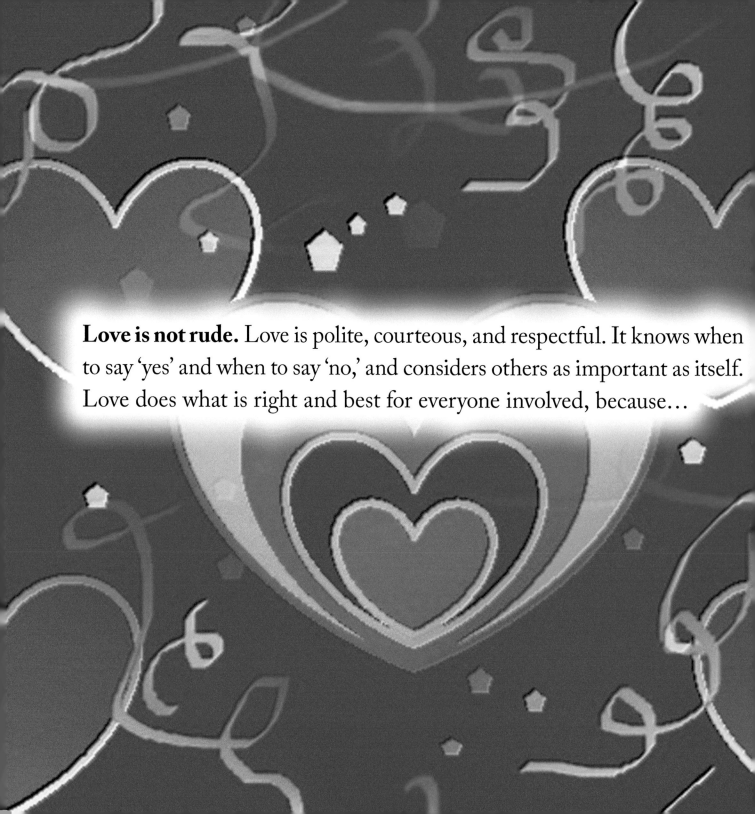

Love is not rude. Love is polite, courteous, and respectful. It knows when to say 'yes' and when to say 'no,' and considers others as important as itself. Love does what is right and best for everyone involved, because…

…Love is not selfish.

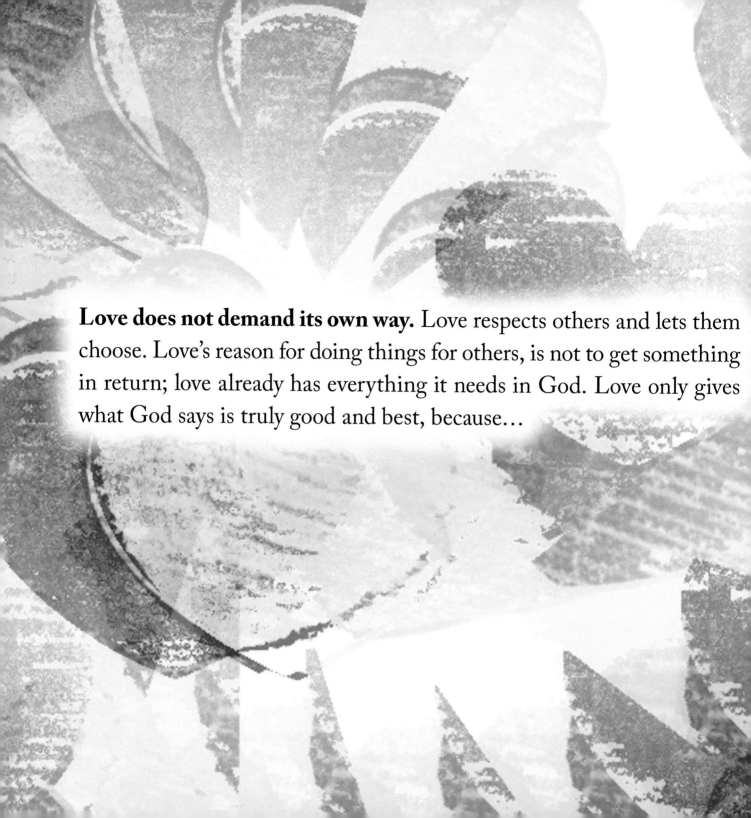

Love does not demand its own way. Love respects others and lets them choose. Love's reason for doing things for others, is not to get something in return; love already has everything it needs in God. Love only gives what God says is truly good and best, because…

...Love is not selfish.

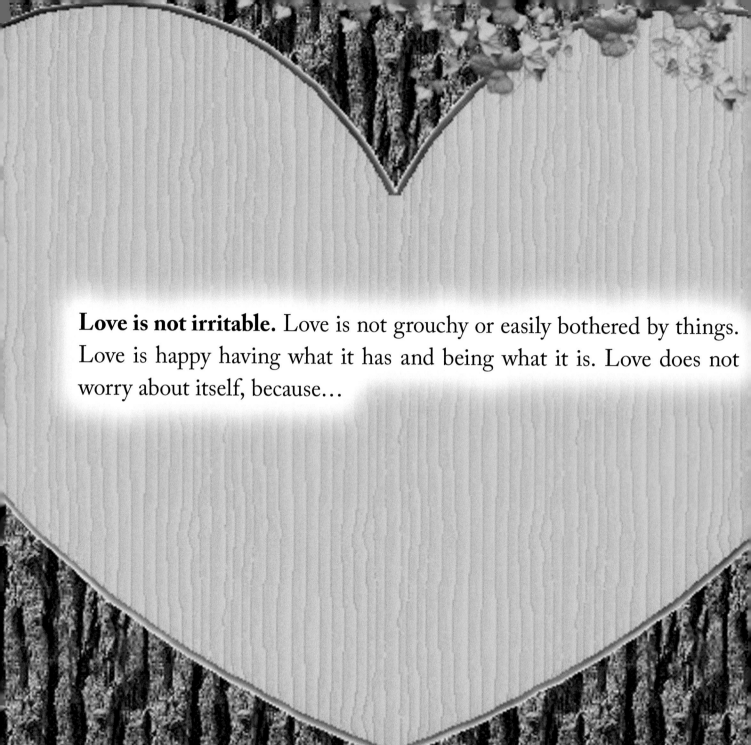

Love is not irritable. Love is not grouchy or easily bothered by things. Love is happy having what it has and being what it is. Love does not worry about itself, because…

…Love is not selfish.

Love does not keep a record of wrongs. Love forgives and is understanding, because…

…Love is not selfish.

Love does not rejoice about injustice, but rejoices whenever the truth wins out. Love is never happy when someone is treated unfairly, but it is always happy when the truth makes things right again, because…

…Love is not selfish.

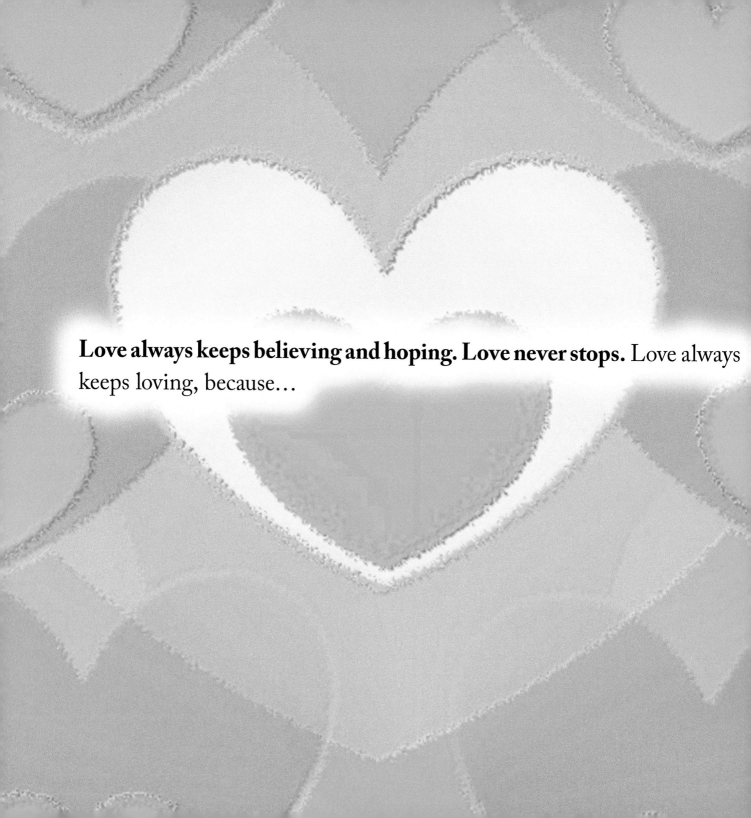

Love always keeps believing and hoping. Love never stops. Love always keeps loving, because…

…Love is not selfish.

"Hi, again! We hope you have enjoyed learning more about love today, and how selfishness prevents us from really loving one another.

The bible tells us in 1 John 4:8 (NLT) that **"...God is love."** Love is what God does. It is His character and very nature. Love is not a feeling or an emotion. Love is action.

God is always patient and kind toward you. He is always happy to see you blessed and has even more blessings to share with you than you could ever imagine! God is always honest with you. He is polite, courteous, and respectful toward you. You are very important to Him. God respects you and that is why He has given you freedom to choose. God's love for you never ends. He always has and always will love you—no matter what!"

"God loves you because of Who He is. Only He can love you perfectly at all times. You can always depend on Him.

The bible instructs us to:

"Be imitators of God, therefore, as dearly loved children and live a life of love…"
Ephesians 5:1&2 (NIV).

When we know God's love for us, we have the honor of loving, too!"

Printed in the United States
by Baker & Taylor Publisher Services